W9-CKI-337

PRO FOOTBALL'S
DREAM TEAMS

by Michael Sandler

Consultant: Norries Wilson
Head Football Coach
Columbia University

BEARPORT
PUBLISHING

New York, New York

Credits

Cover and Title Page, © Joe Robbins/Getty Images; TOCL, © Tomasso DeRosa/Corbis; TOCR, © Scott Audette/Reuters/Landov; 4T, © SportsChrome/Newscom; 4B, © Pierre Ducharme/Reuters/Landov; 5T, © Kevin Reece/Icon SMI/Newscom; 5B, © Scott Audette/ Reuters/Landov; 6, © KRT/Newscom; 7, © Gary Wiepert/Reuters/Landov; 8, © AP Images/Winslow Townson; 9, © SportsChrome/Newscom; 10, © KRT/Newscom; 11, © Harry How/Getty Images; 12, © AP Images/Tom Uhlman; 13, © Justin Lane/EPA/Corbis; 14, © KRT/Newscom; 15, © Tomasso DeRosa/Corbis; 16, © AP Images/AJ Mast; 17, © Al Pereira/Getty Images; 18, © KRT/Newscom; 19, © Ezra Shaw/Getty Images; 20, © AP Images/Ben Liebenberg; 21, © Tom Hauck/Getty Images; 22TL, © Tomasso DeRosa/ Corbis; 22TR, © Scott Audette/Reuters/Landov; 22CL, © Marc Serota/Reuters/Landov; 22CR, © AP Images/David Drapkin; 22BL, © Gary Hershorn/Reuters/Landov; 22BR, © Tannen Maury/EPA/Landov.

Publisher: Kenn Goin
Senior Editor: Lisa Wiseman
Creative Director: Spencer Brinker
Design: Keith Plechaty
Photo Researcher: Jennifer Bright

*All stats and records are current through the 2009–2010 season.

Library of Congress Cataloging-in-Publication Data

Sandler, Michael, 1965-
  Pro football's dream teams / by Michael Sandler ; consultant: Norries Wilson.
      p. cm. — (Football-o-rama)
  Includes bibliographical references and index.
  ISBN-13: 978-1-936088-24-9 (library binding)
  ISBN-10: 1-936088-24-X (library binding)
  1. Football teams—United States—History—Juvenile literature. I. Wilson, Norries. II. Title.
  GV954.S26 2010
  796.332'64—dc22

                              2010015527

For more information, write to Bearport Publishing Company, Inc., 101 Fifth Avenue, Suite 6R, New York, New York 10003. Printed in the United States of America in North Mankato, Minnesota.

022011
021011CGC

10 9 8 7 6 5 4 3 2

CONTENTS

DREAM TEAMS

In the NFL, success can come quickly, but it can also disappear just as fast. One season, a team may be a Super Bowl **contender**. The next, it might not even make the playoffs. Injuries and **free agency** are two reasons why keeping a winning group together isn't easy.

New England Patriots quarterback Tom Brady (#12) hands off the ball to running back Corey Dillon (#28) during Super Bowl XXXIX (39).

Pittsburgh Steelers kicker Jeff Reed (#3) kicks a field goal as his teammates hold back the Arizona Cardinals during Super Bowl XLIII (43).

A few **franchises**, however, have found the secrets to long-term success—winning combinations of players, coaches, and **strategies**. Year after year, these teams are always right at the top of the pack. In this book, you will read about four of these clubs—the New England Patriots, the Pittsburgh Steelers, the Indianapolis Colts, and the New Orleans Saints. It will be easy to see why they have ruled the league for the last decade and are considered the dream teams of the NFL.

Quarterback Peyton Manning (#18) looks to hand off the ball to Indianapolis Colts running back Joseph Addai (#29) during Super Bowl XLI (41).

New Orleans Saints cornerback Tracy Porter (#22) runs for a touchdown during Super Bowl XLIV (44).

THE NEW ENGLAND PATRIOTS

First Season: 1960 (as the Boston Patriots; renamed the New England Patriots in 1971)

Super Bowl Appearances: 6

Super Bowl Wins: 3

Playoff Appearances from 2000–2009: 7

Starting Quarterback: Tom Brady

Head Coach: Bill Belichick

For nearly a decade, the New England Patriots have stood in the way of any NFL team with hopes of winning a **title**. Since 2001, they have had a winning record every single year and have had three Super Bowl victories along the way.

Even in the years when they failed to win the title, New England played incredibly well. In 2007, for example, the Patriots became the first NFL team to go undefeated in a 16-game regular season. That year, they didn't just beat the other teams—they crushed them. They rolled over the Washington Redskins in a 52-7 victory. They destroyed the Buffalo Bills in a 56-10 win. In four separate games, they scored 48 points or more.

The Patriots show no signs of giving up their winning ways. In 2009, they won the **AFC East division** title for the seventh time in nine years.

HIGHLIGHTS

2001–02	Defeated the St. Louis Rams, 20-17, in Super Bowl XXXVI (36)
2003–04	Defeated the Carolina Panthers, 32-29, in Super Bowl XXXVIII (38)
2004–05	Defeated the Philadelphia Eagles, 24-21, in Super Bowl XXXIX (39)
2007–08	Won a record 16 regular-season NFL games

New England Patriots wide receiver Randy Moss (#81) avoids a tackle during the Patriots 56-10 win over the Buffalo Bills.

SECRETS OF THE PATRIOTS' SUCCESS

What are the secrets of New England's success? It all comes down to two men—head coach Bill Belichick and quarterback Tom Brady.

Coach Belichick has a strict **philosophy** that emphasizes not the individual players but the team as a whole. Every player must put the team's needs first. In practice, if one person makes a mistake, the whole team may have to run laps around the field as punishment. The hard work pays off on game days, though. No team is better prepared than the Patriots.

There's only one exception to Belichick's team-first philosophy. On-field leader Tom Brady is more important than the other players. Why? His strong arm and sharp passes to **receivers** such as Randy Moss are what keep New England winning each and every year.

Coach Bill Belichick talks to his defense during a game.

Tom Brady during Super Bowl XXXIX (39)

For Tom Brady and the Patriots, the victory in Super Bowl XXXIX (39) was extra sweet. They became only the second team in NFL history to win three Super Bowls in four years. The other team was the Dallas Cowboys in the 1990s.

THE PITTSBURGH STEELERS

First Season: 1933 (as the Pittsburgh Pirates; renamed the Pittsburgh Steelers in 1940)

Super Bowl Appearances: 7

Super Bowl Wins: 6

Playoff Appearances from 2000–2009: 6

Starting Quarterback: Ben Roethlisberger

Head Coach: Mike Tomlin

No NFL team has a prouder or more glorious history than the Pittsburgh Steelers. Pittsburgh began winning Super Bowls in the 1970s. During the last ten years, they've won the big game twice. In Super Bowl XL (40) in February 2006, the Steelers easily defeated the Seattle Seahawks, 21-10, behind the heroic play of receiver Hines Ward.

Then in Super Bowl XLIII (43) in February 2009, the Steelers beat Kurt Warner and the Arizona Cardinals. This was the sixth Super Bowl victory in the team's history and the most of any NFL team. During this game, another receiver, Santonio Holmes, helped seal the 27-23 win. His biggest play came with just half a minute left in the game. Santonio extended his arms to make an amazing touchdown catch in the corner of the **end zone**.

HIGHLIGHTS

| 2005-06 | Defeated the Seattle Seahawks, 21-10, in Super Bowl XL (40) |
| 2008-09 | Defeated the Arizona Cardinals, 27-23, in Super Bowl XLIII (43) |

Hines Ward (#86) scores a touchdown during the fourth quarter of Super Bowl XL (40).

SECRETS OF THE STEELERS' SUCCESS

What are the secrets of the Steelers' success? **Stability** is a big factor. Many NFL teams swap head coaches every few seasons. The Steelers have had just three over the last 40 years—Chuck Noll, Bill Cowher, and, current coach, Mike Tomlin.

Another reason for the team's success is that they have a fierce, punishing defense that makes it very difficult for other teams to score. When Chuck Noll was coach, he set up a defense that became known as the Steel Curtain. This defense was so strong that it felt like there was a metal wall between the other teams and the end zone.

Coach Tomlin has maintained Noll's emphasis on stopping teams from scoring. Today, star defenders such as **linebacker** James Harrison and **safety** Troy Polamalu keep the Steelers' defense amongst the NFL's finest. Combined with a strong passing game led by quarterback Ben Roethlisberger, it makes Pittsburgh very tough to beat.

Troy Polamalu (#43) tackles Cincinnati Bengals wide receiver Chad Ochocinco (#85) during a game in 2008.

James Harrison (#92) runs downfield for a 100-yard (91-m) touchdown in Super Bowl XLIII (43).

Defense was key to the Steelers' Super Bowl XLIII (43) victory, with James Harrison making the biggest defensive play in the game. He **intercepted** Arizona Cardinals quarterback Kurt Warner's pass and ran it back 100 yards (91 m) for a first-half touchdown. It was the longest play in Super Bowl history.

THE INDIANAPOLIS COLTS

First Season: 1953 (as the Baltimore Colts; moved to Indianapolis in 1984)

Super Bowl Appearances: 4

Super Bowl Wins: 2

Playoff Appearances from 2000–2009: 9

Starting Quarterback: Peyton Manning

Head Coach: Jim Caldwell

Since 2000, the Indianapolis Colts have had an amazing record. In the past ten years, they have missed the playoffs only once, back in 2001.

Offense—and lots of it—is the name of the game for the Colts. They score quickly and often. Usually the team doesn't use a huddle. Instead, quarterback Peyton Manning calls the plays right at the **line of scrimmage**. Most teams use a **no-huddle** offense only when they are running out of time. The Colts, however, use it all game long. The benefit? It doesn't allow the opposing defense time to prepare for the play.

The Colts' speedy offense shows no signs of slowing down. In 2009, Indianapolis won its first 14 games and moved on to its second Super Bowl appearance of the decade.

HIGHLIGHTS

2003-04	Reached the **AFC Championship Game**
2006-07	Defeated the Chicago Bears, 29-17, in Super Bowl XLI (41)
2009-10	Made their eighth straight playoff appearance; advanced to Super Bowl XLIV (44)

Peyton Manning calls a play at the line of scrimmage during Super Bowl XLI (41).

SECRETS OF THE COLTS' SUCCESS

What is the secret of the Colts' success? Without question it's Peyton Manning, the world's best quarterback. He is the only player ever to be named the NFL's Most Valuable Player (MVP) four times. No other passer inspires such fear in members of the opposing team's defense.

Aside from his amazing arm, it's Peyton's ability to score touchdowns so quickly that sets him apart from other quarterbacks. No opposing team's lead is ever safe against the Colts—no matter how big—with Peyton in the game. Just give him the ball and a few minutes to work, and Peyton can bring his team to victory.

Of course, working this last-minute magic is possible only with talented teammates to catch Peyton's passes. Star receivers such as Reggie Wayne, Marvin Harrison (through 2008), Dallas Clark, and Pierre Garcon have also been extremely important to the Colts' success.

Reggie Wayne reaches out to catch a pass in a game against the Jacksonville Jaguars in 2009.

Peyton Manning looks to pass the ball during the AFC Championship Game against the New York Jets.

The AFC Championship Game against the New York Jets in January 2010 was typical for the Colts. They fell behind, 17-6. Then, with just four quick passes and a minute left in the first half, Peyton took the Colts downfield and produced a touchdown. He threw two more touchdown passes in the second half to give Indianapolis a 30-17 victory and a trip to Super Bowl XLIV (44).

THE NEW ORLEANS SAINTS

First Season: 1967
Super Bowl Appearances: 1
Super Bowl Wins: 1
Playoff Appearances from 2000-2009: 3

Starting Quarterback:
Drew Brees
Head Coach:
Sean Payton

If the Steelers, the Patriots, and the Colts have ruled the NFL for the last ten years, then the New Orleans Saints look ready to take over as the league's newest super team. New Orleans finally reached football's highest level during the 2009–2010 season. They won their first 13 games behind the league's highest scoring offense. Then they marched through the playoffs and right into Super Bowl XLIV (44).

In that game, New Orleans had to face the mighty Peyton Manning and the Indianapolis Colts, the NFL's winningest team. Surprising many, they overcame the Colts, 31-17, to win the first Super Bowl in team history.

HIGHLIGHTS

2006–07	Made the playoffs for the first time in six years; reached the **NFC Championship Game**
2009–10	Defeated the Indianapolis Colts, 31-17, in Super Bowl XLIV (44)

Jeremy Shockey (#88) celebrates after scoring a touchdown in Super Bowl XLIV (44).

SECRETS OF THE SAINTS' SUCCESS

What are the secrets of the Saints' success? It all boils down to two key moves that the team made in 2006. That year, New Orleans brought in a new coach, Sean Payton, and a new quarterback, Drew Brees.

Despite a terrible season in 2005—the Saints went 3-13—Coach Payton told his players that they were contenders for the title. The players took his words to heart and the team advanced to the NFC Championship Game.

Drew Brees's fast-paced scoring attack is a big reason for the Saints' **turnaround**. Drew, the league's most accurate quarterback, is helped by teammates such as **versatile** receiver and running back Reggie Bush. Reggie can turn any play from a **pass reception** to a **punt return** into a **breakaway** touchdown. With a talented defense to match the offense, the Saints are likely to remain a dream team for years to come.

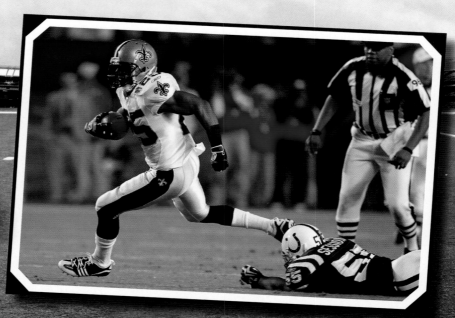

Reggie Bush (#25) breaks away from Colts linebacker Clint Session (#55) in Super Bowl XLIV (44).

Drew Brees in action during Super Bowl XLIV (44)

Super Bowl XLIV (44) was the biggest game in New Orleans football history. Throughout the game, Drew was simply exceptional. He completed 32 of 39 passes for 288 yards (263 m) and 2 touchdowns. Afterward, Drew was named Super Bowl MVP.

The New England Patriots

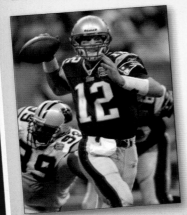

Year	Wins	Losses
2009:	10	6
2008:	11	5
2007:	16	0
2006:	12	4
2005:	10	6
*2004:	14	2
*2003:	14	2
2002:	9	7
*2001:	11	5
2000:	5	11

The Indianapolis Colts

Year	Wins	Losses
2009:	14	2
2008:	12	4
2007:	13	3
*2006:	12	4
2005:	14	2
2004:	12	4
2003:	12	4
2002:	10	6
2001:	6	10
2000:	10	6

The Pittsburgh Steelers

Year	Wins	Losses
2009:	9	7
*2008:	12	4
2007:	10	6
2006:	8	8
*2005:	11	5
2004:	15	1
2003:	6	10
2002:	10	5
2001:	13	3
2000:	9	7

The New Orleans Saints

Year	Wins	Losses
*2009:	13	3
2008:	8	8
2007:	7	9
2006:	10	6
2005:	3	13
2004:	8	8
2003:	8	8
2002:	9	7
2001:	7	9
2000:	10	6

* the season the team
won the Super Bowl

GLOSSARY

AFC Championship Game (AY-EFF-CEE CHAM-pee-uhn-*ship* GAME) a playoff game that decides which American Football Conference (AFC) team will go to the Super Bowl

AFC East division (AY-EFF-CEE EEST di-VIZH-uhn) one of four divisions in the NFL's American Football Conference (AFC)

breakaway (BRAYK-uh-way) a play in which the ball carrier breaks free from defenders and runs down the field untouched

contender (kuhn-TEND-ur) a team that has a chance of winning a big game

end zone (END ZOHN) the area at either end of a football field where touchdowns are scored

franchises (FRAN-chize-iz) teams, clubs

free agency (FREE AY-juhn-see) the ability for players to leave one team and choose to play for another

intercepted (in-tur-SEP-tid) caught a pass meant for a player on the other team

line of scrimmage (LINE UHV SKRIM-ij) an imaginary line across the field where the ball is put at the beginning of a play

linebacker (LINE-bak-ur) a defensive player who lines up behind the line of scrimmage, makes tackles, and puts pressure on quarterbacks

NFC Championship Game (EN-EFF-SEE CHAM-pee-uhn-*ship* GAME) a playoff game that decides which National Football Conference (NFC) team will go to the Super Bowl

no-huddle (NOH-HUHD-uhl) when the offense quickly lines up at the line of scrimmage without meeting in a huddle to discuss the play first

offense (AW-fenss) scoring points; the part of a game in which a team is trying to score

pass reception (PASS ri-SEP-shuhn) a pass that is caught by an offensive player

philosophy (fuh-LOSS-uh-fee) a way of thinking

punt return (PUHNT ri-TURN) the attempt of a player to run the ball up field after he catches a ball kicked by the other team

receivers (ri-SEE-vurz) players whose job it is to catch passes

safety (SAYF-tee) a defensive player who lines up farthest behind the line of scrimmage, covers receivers, and tackles ball carriers who get past other defensive players

stability (stuh-BIL-i-tee) a period of time without a lot of change

strategies (STRAT-uh-jeez) the plans and plays a team uses to score points or stop other teams from scoring

title (TYE-tuhl) the championship

turnaround (TURN-uh-round) to go from playing very poorly one season to very well the next

versatile (VUR-suh-tuhl) useful in many ways

BIBLIOGRAPHY

The Sporting News

USA Today

NFL.com

www.pro-football-reference.com/

READ MORE

Sandler, Michael. *Drew Brees and the New Orleans Saints: Super Bowl XLIV (Super Bowl Superstars)*. New York: Bearport (2011).

Sandler, Michael. *Hines Ward and the Pittsburgh Steelers: Super Bowl XL (Super Bowl Superstars)*. New York: Bearport (2008).

Sandler, Michael. *Peyton Manning and the Indianapolis Colts: Super Bowl XLI (Super Bowl Superstars)*. New York: Bearport (2008).

Sandler, Michael. *Tom Brady and the New England Patriots: Super Bowl XXXVIII (Super Bowl Superstars)*. New York: Bearport (2008).

LEARN MORE ONLINE

To learn more about the NFL's dream teams, visit
www.bearportpublishing.com/FootballORama

INDEX